# MY MUSEUM

a journal for
sketching and collecting

by Lea Redmond

CHRONICLE BOOKS

SAN FRANCISCO

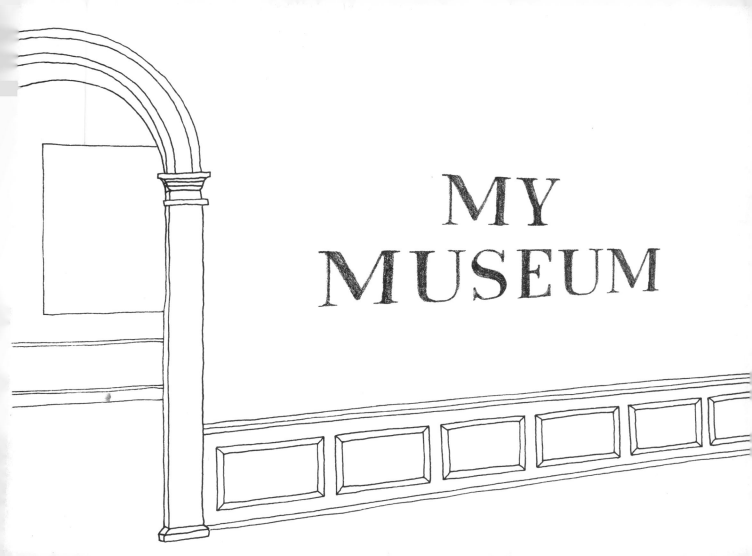

# MY MUSEUM

ISBN 978-1-4521-1534-4

Manufactured in China
Design by Brooke Johnson

10 9 8 7 6 5 4 3 2

Chronicle Books LLC
680 Second Street
San Francisco, CA 94107
www.chroniclebooks.com

As you fill the pages of this journal, it will become your very own personal museum. Draw, paint, or collage a collection of curiosities—things that are beautiful, strange, mundane, or marvelous—into the empty frames and display cases. Use the journal to explore, record, and see the world in new ways. Or fill it with imaginary creatures from your dreams. Create a "memory museum" and curate treasured objects and scenes from your past. Or carry it with you on museum visits, adding your favorite works to your own collection.

The more you look, the more you'll see that all things are museum worthy.

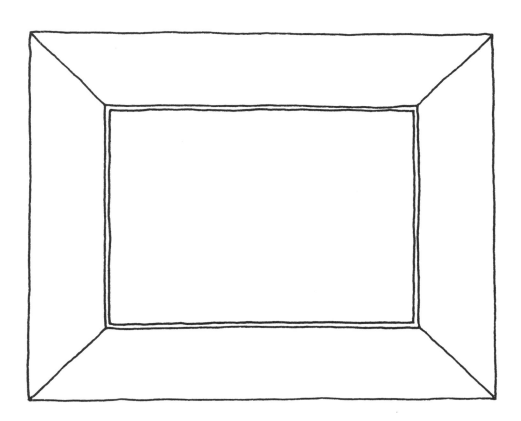

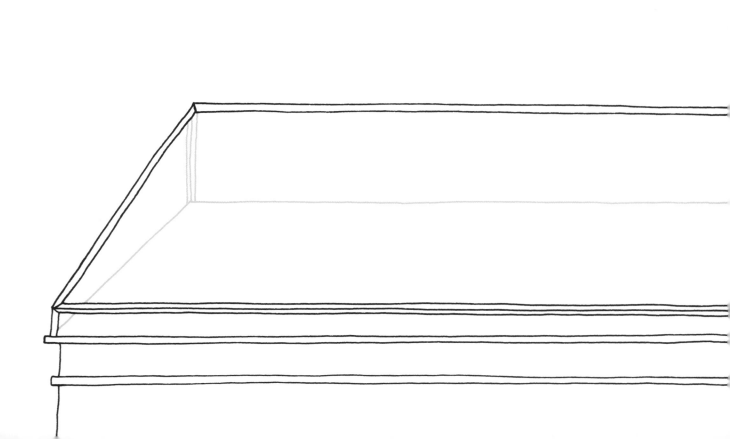

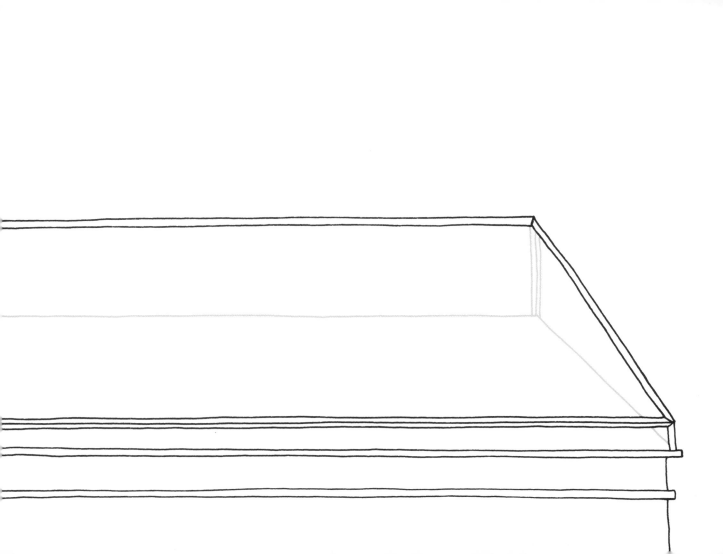

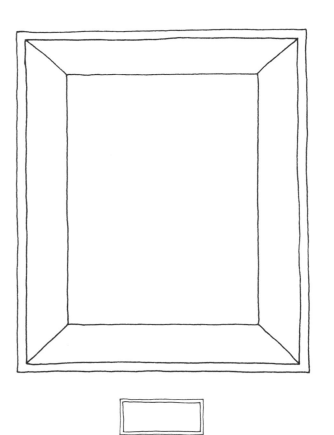

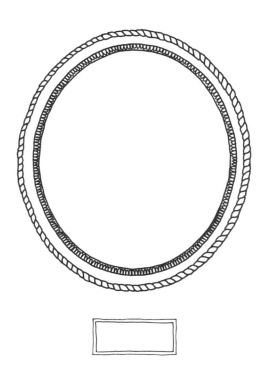

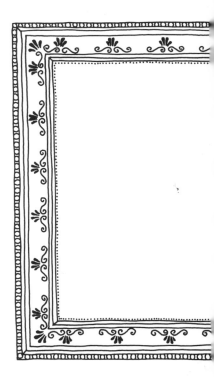

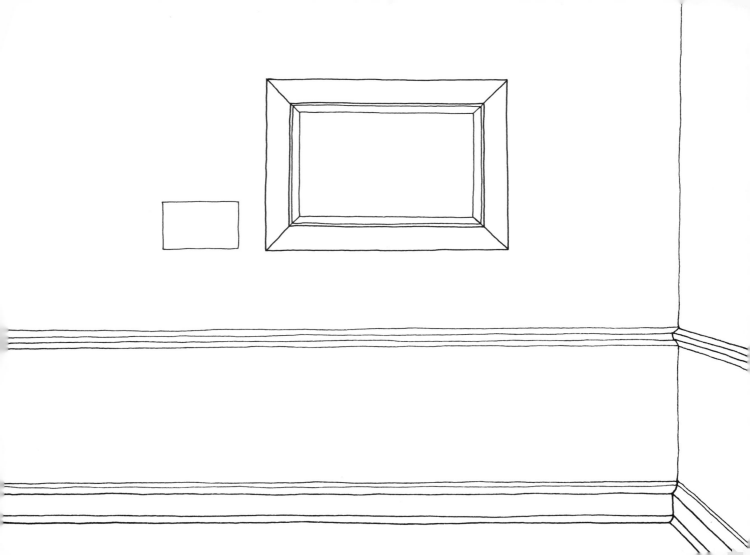

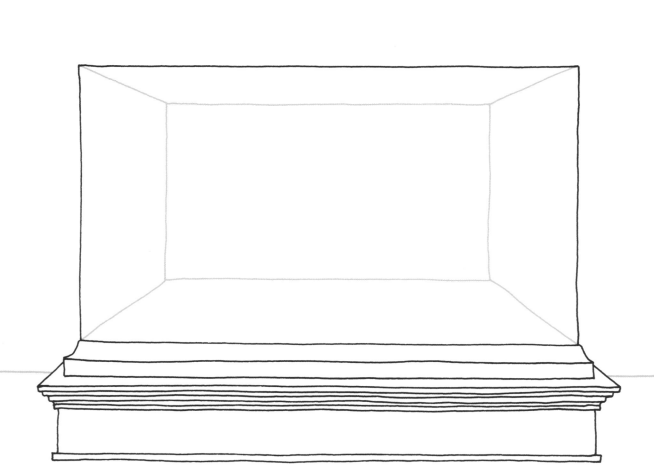

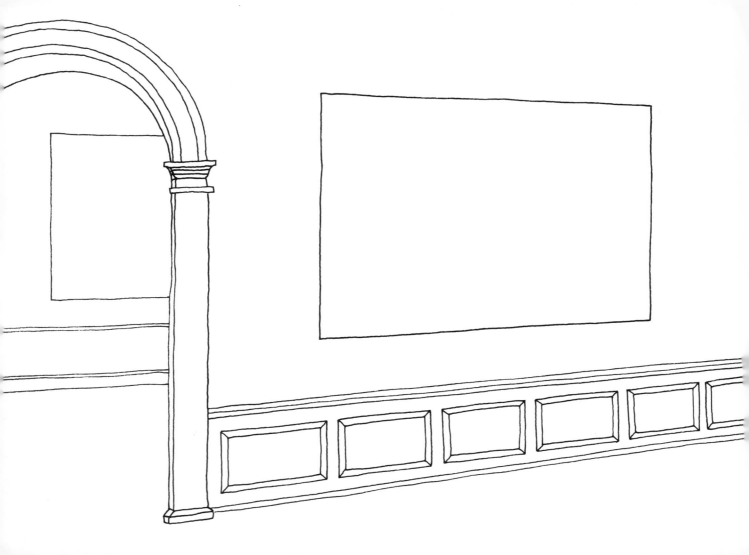

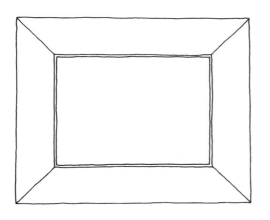
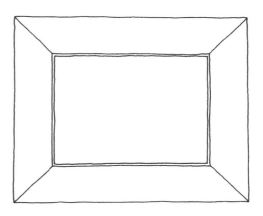

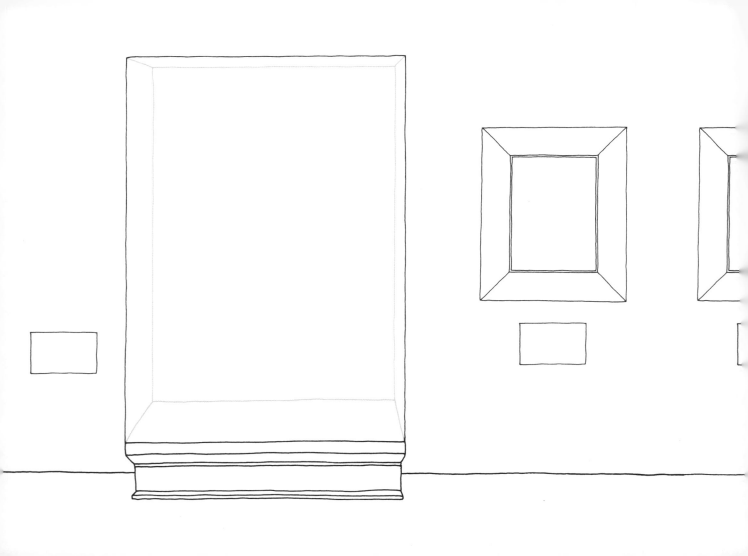

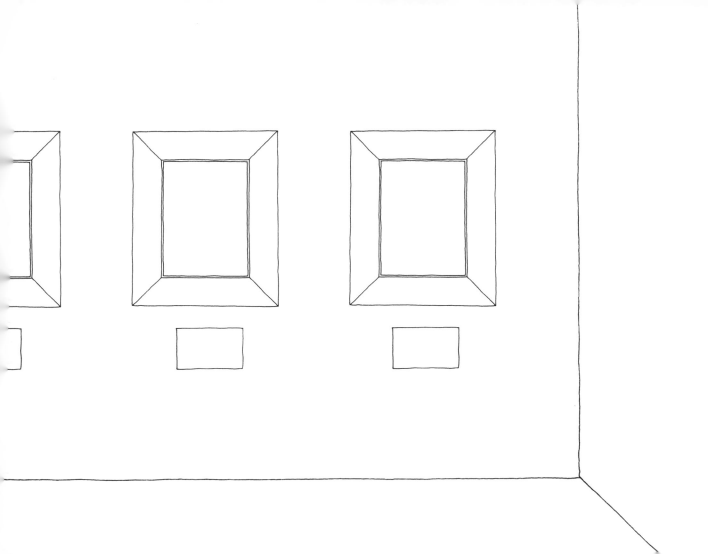

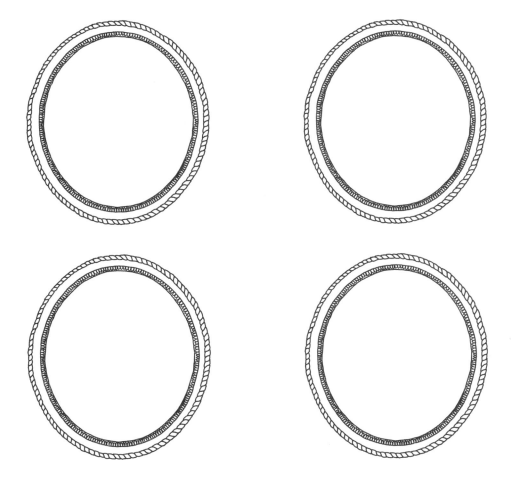

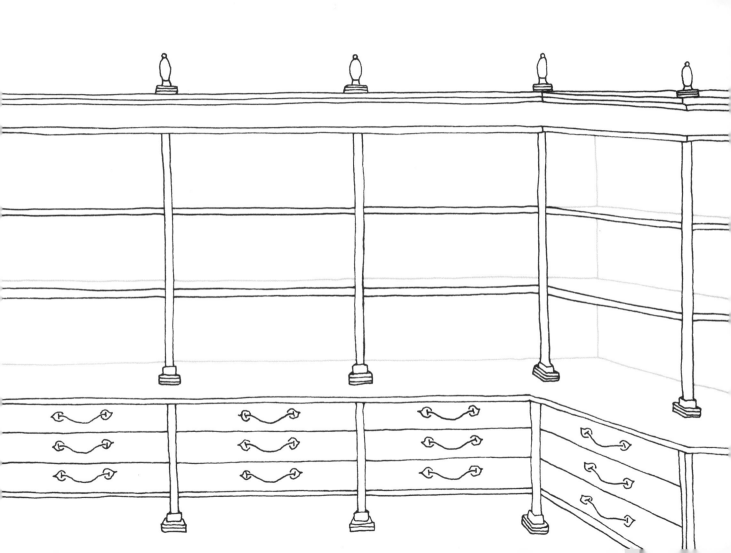

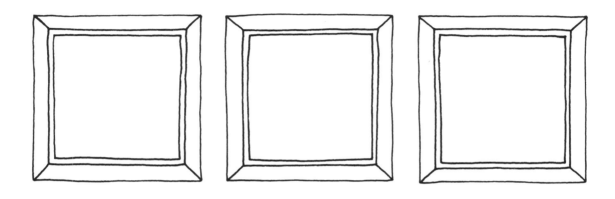

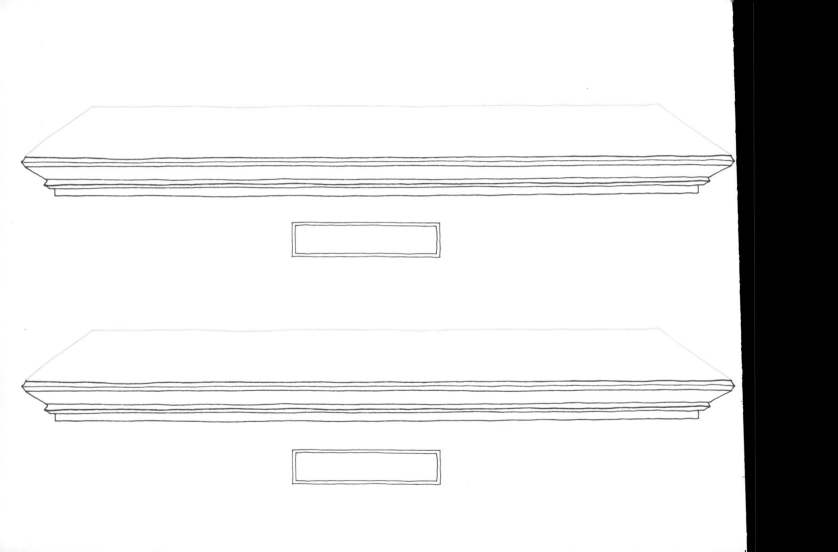

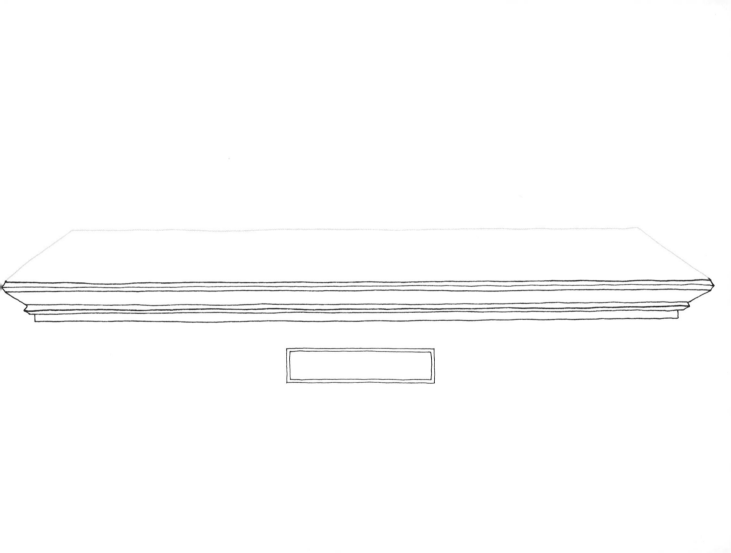

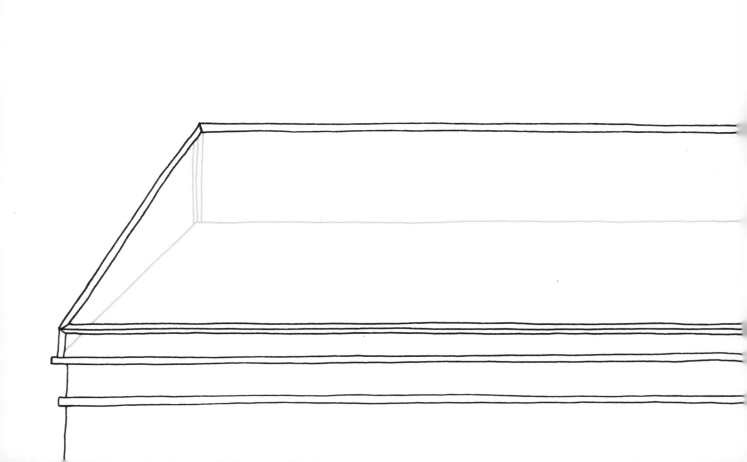

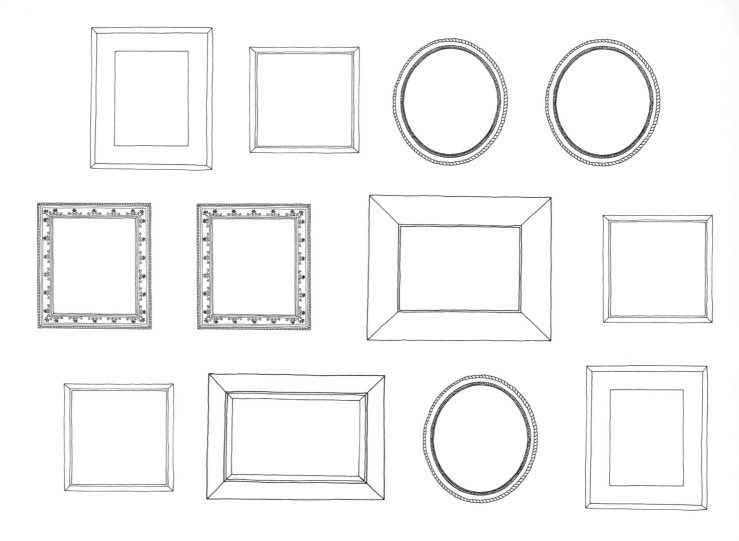

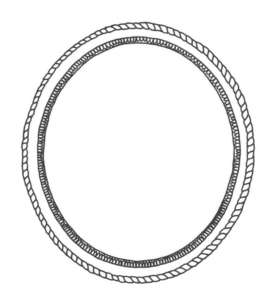

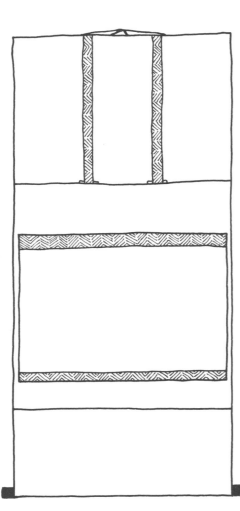
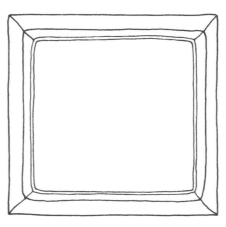

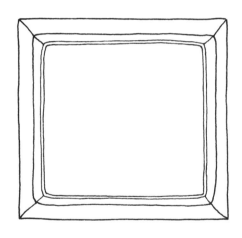
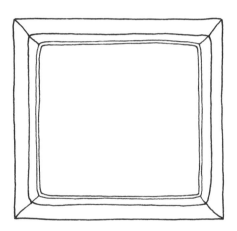

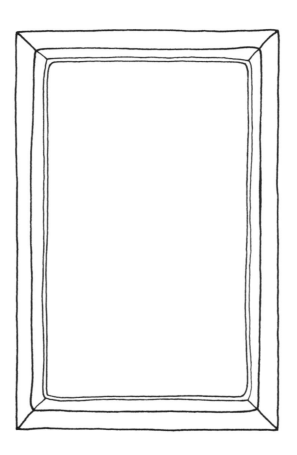

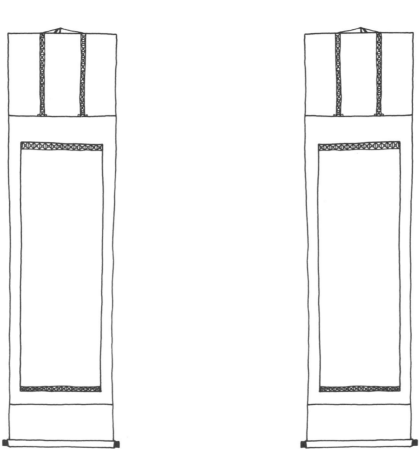

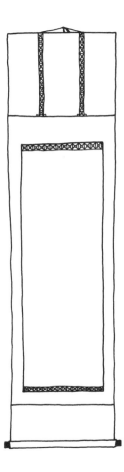
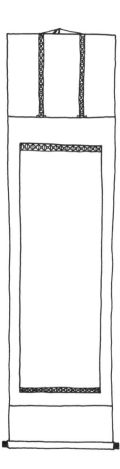

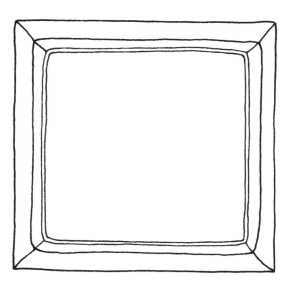

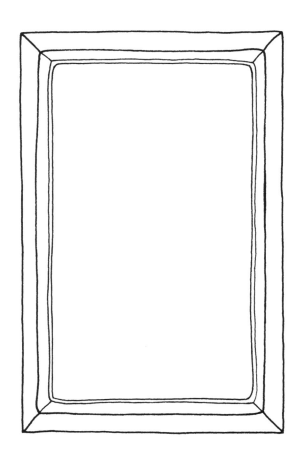

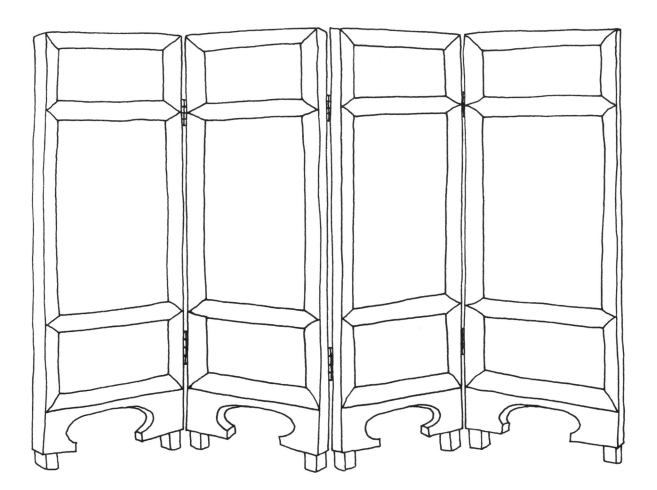

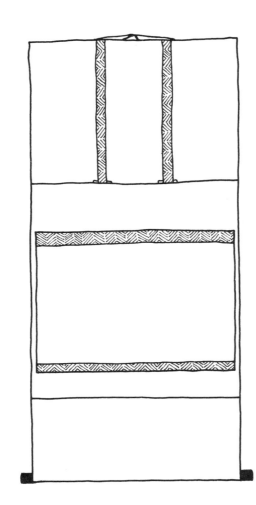

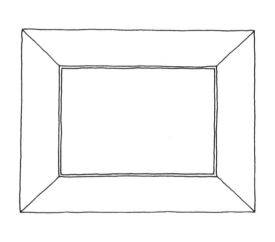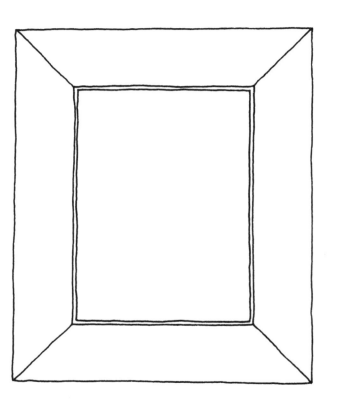

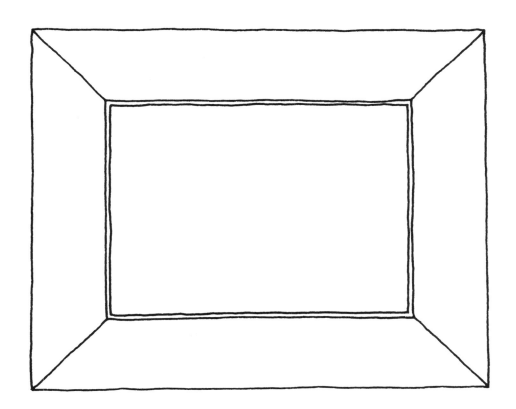

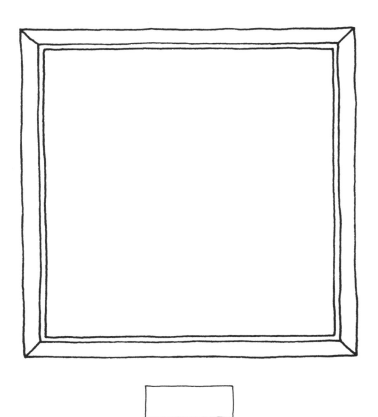

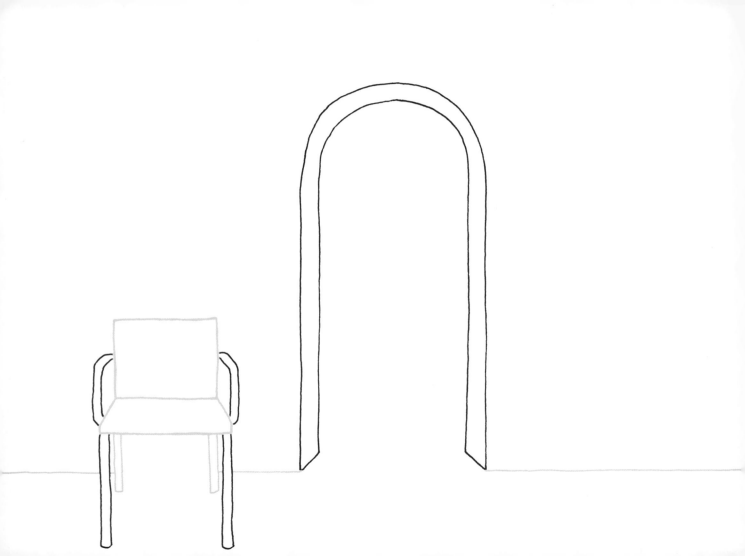

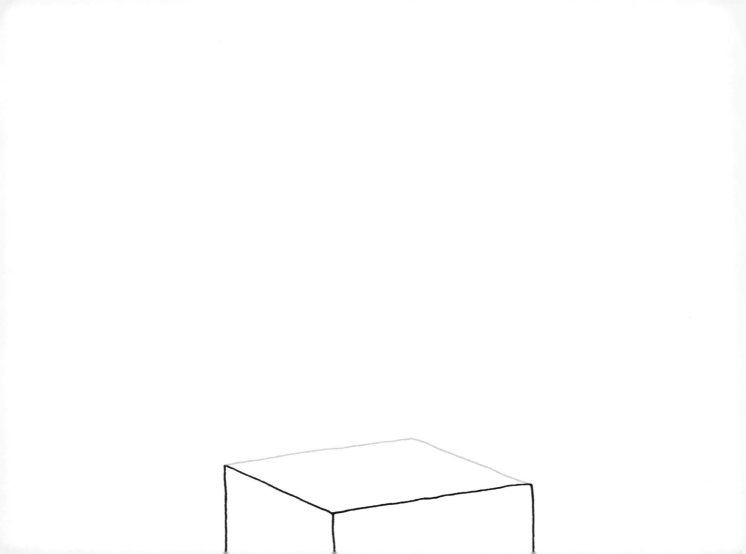

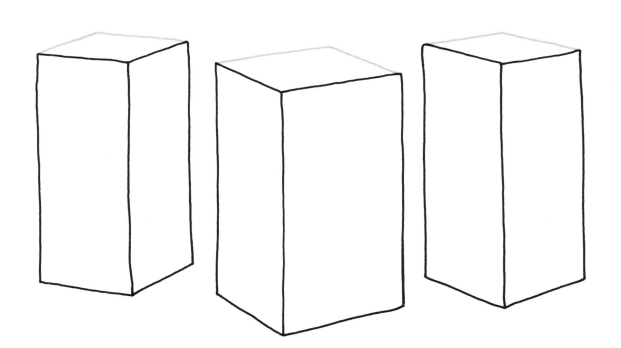

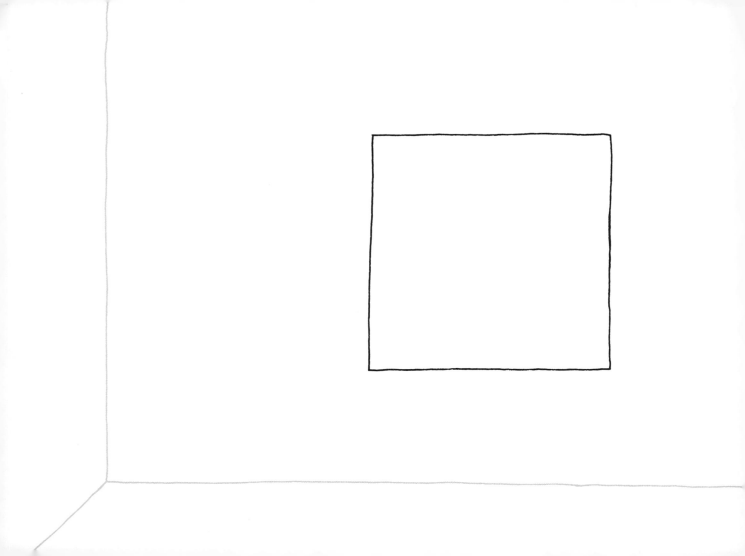

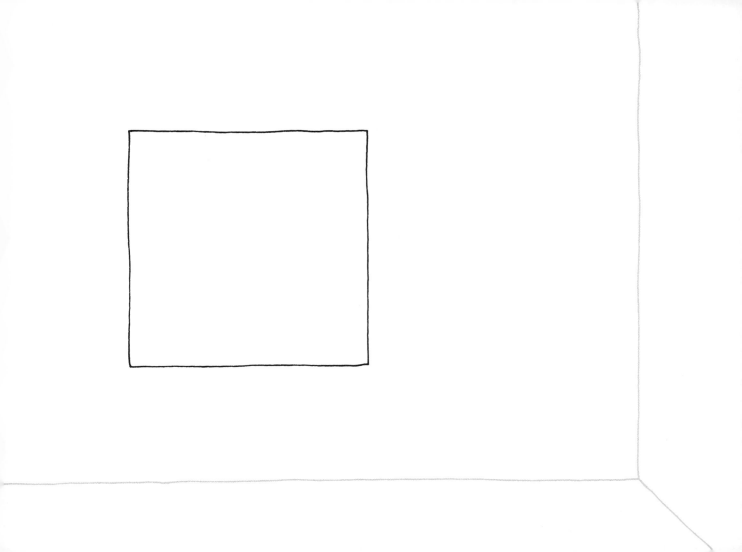

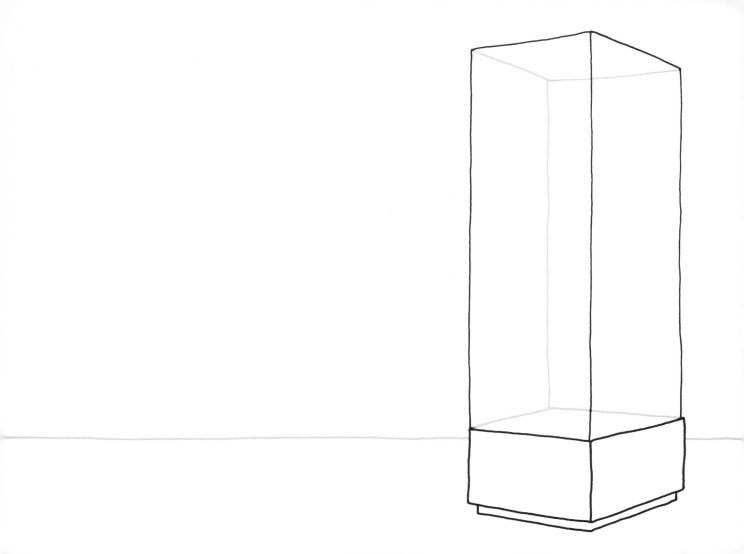

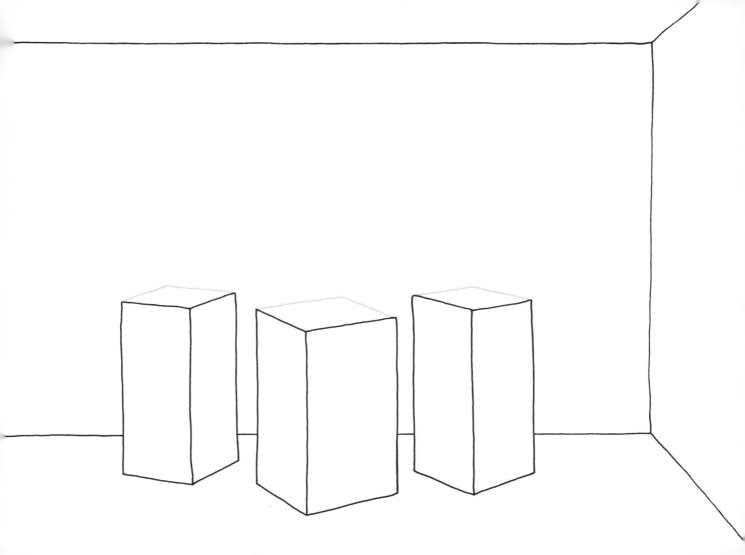

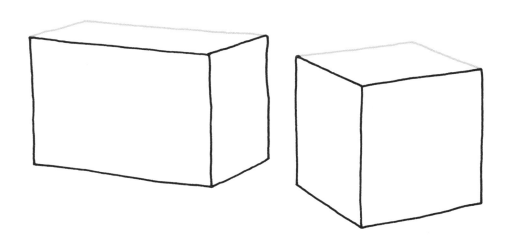

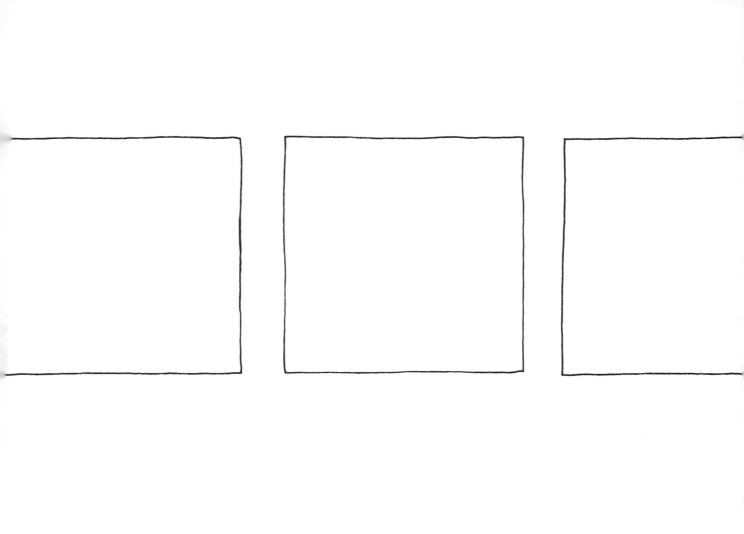

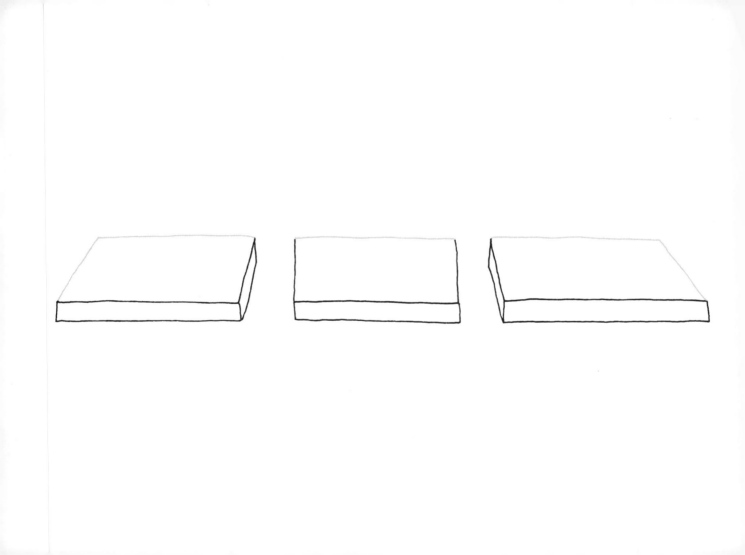

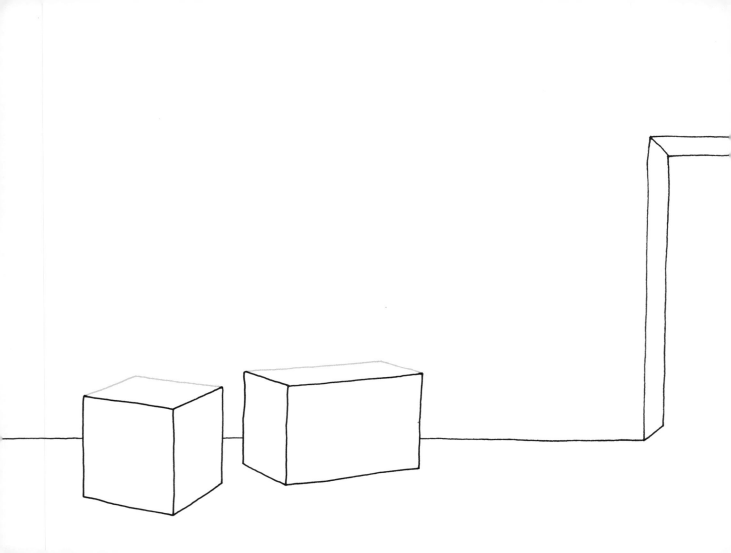

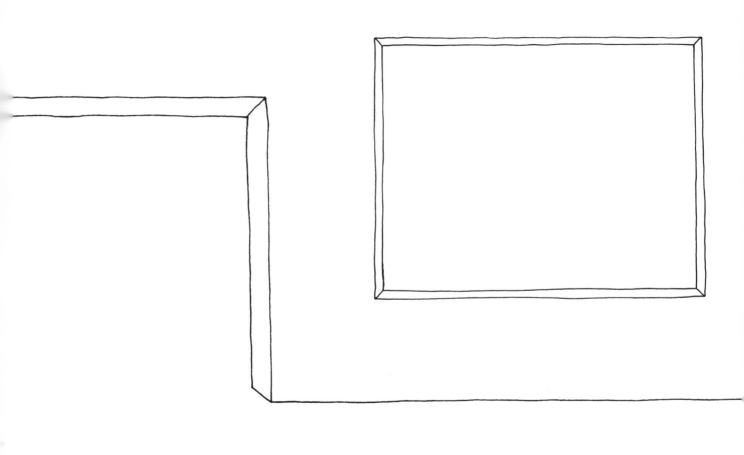

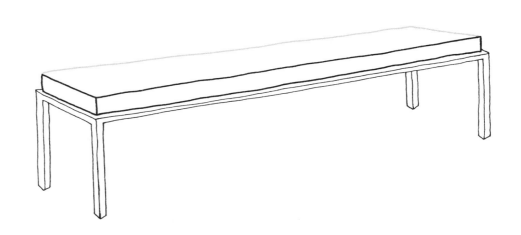

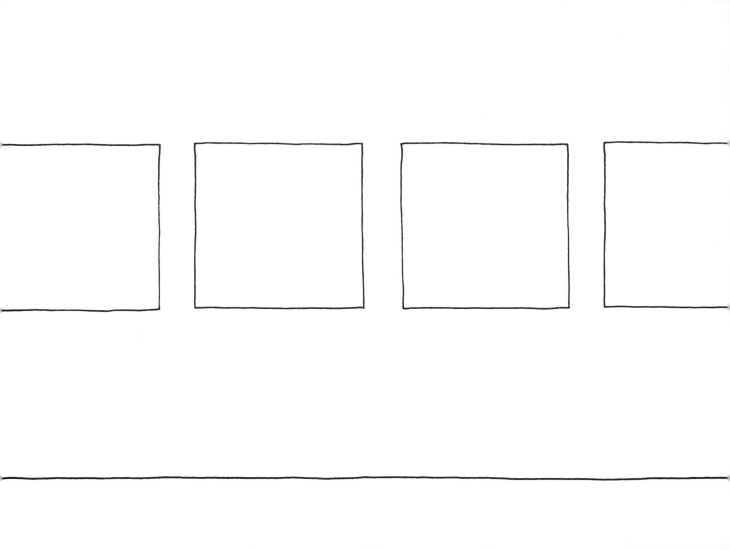

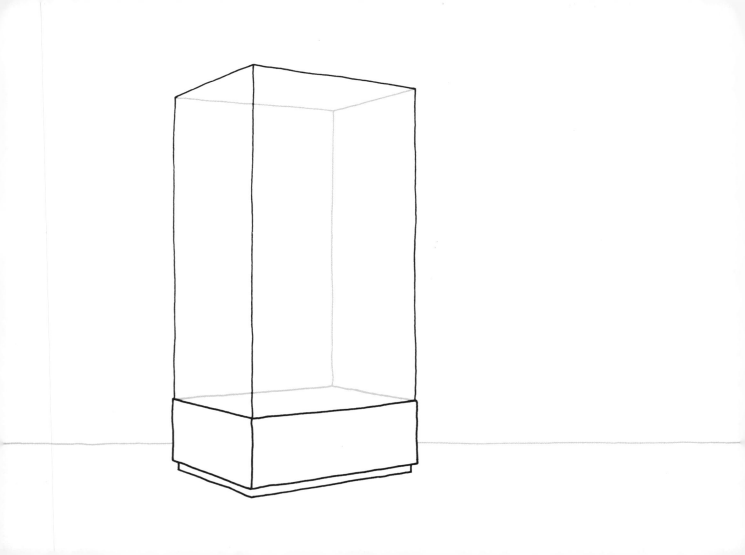

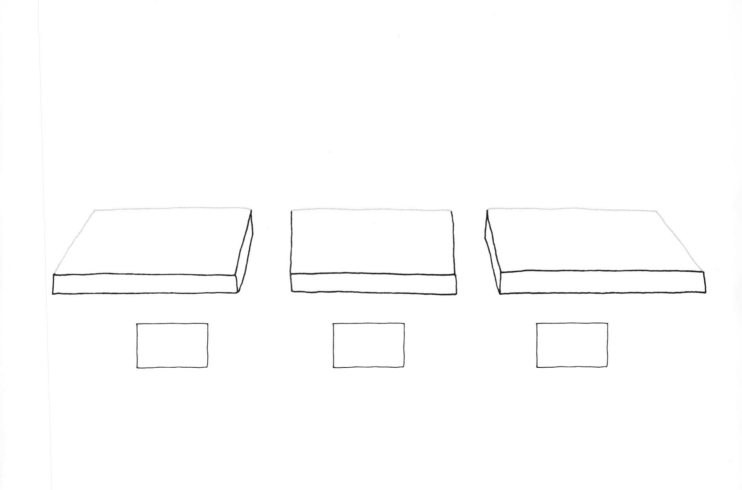

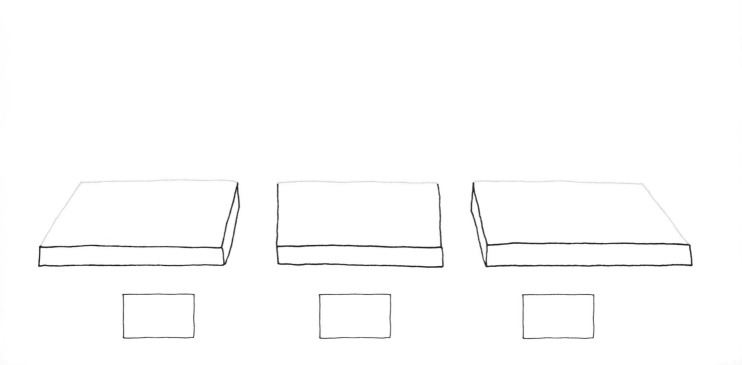

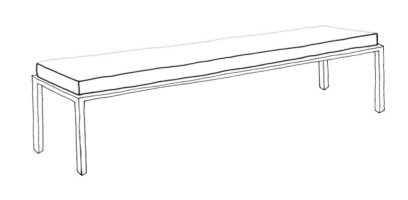

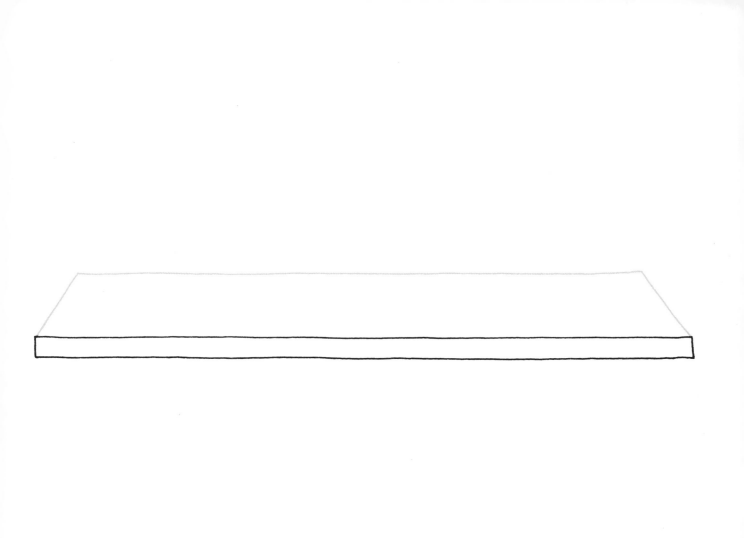

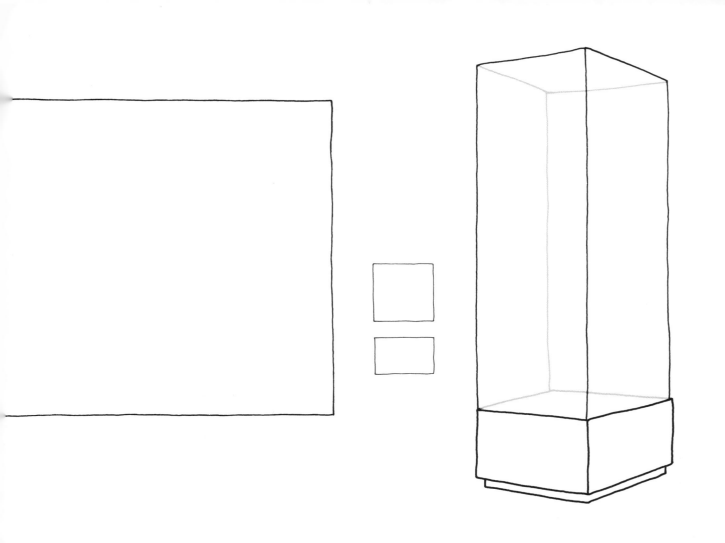

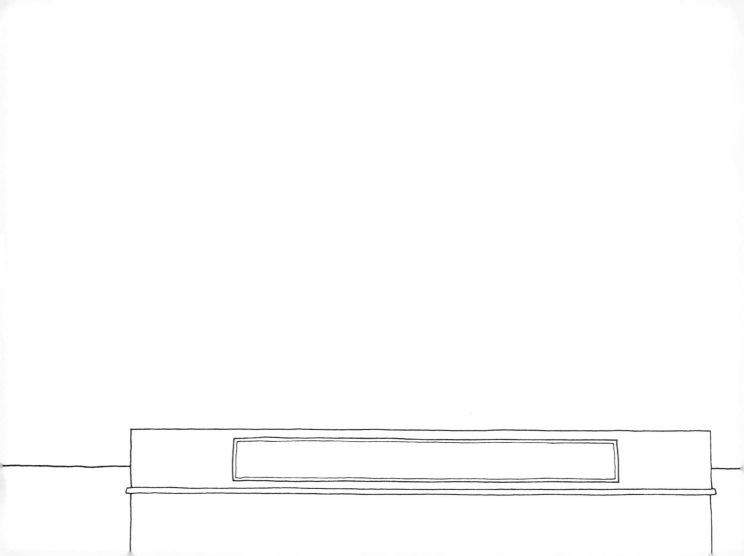

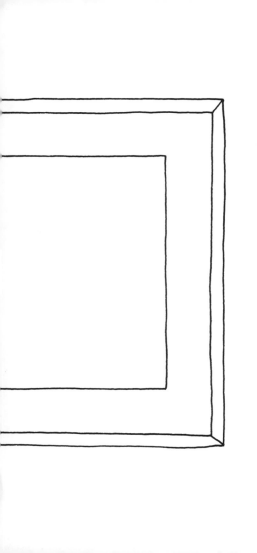

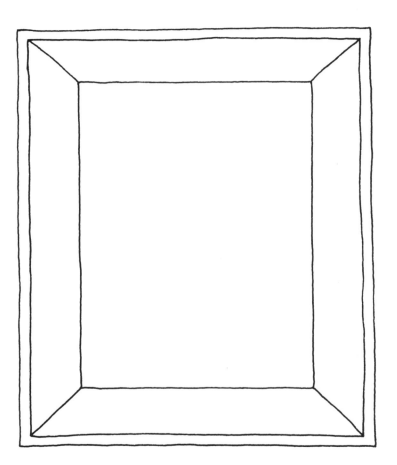

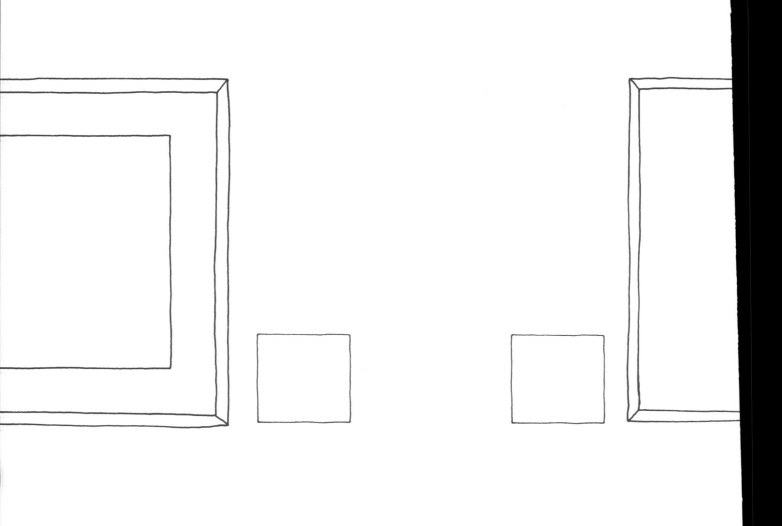

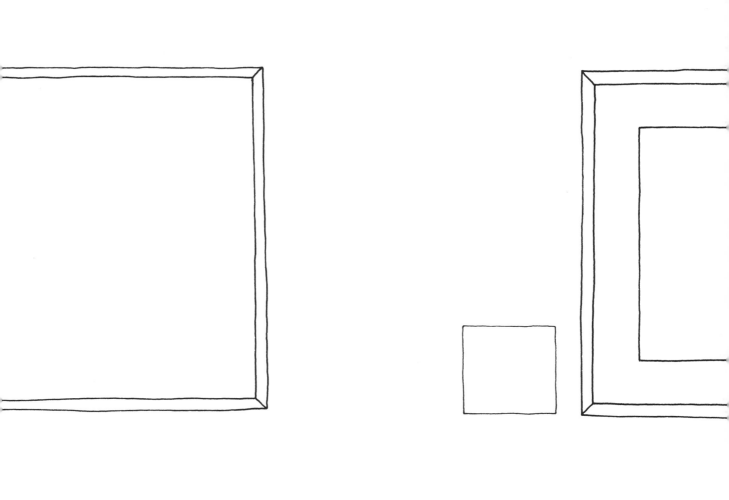

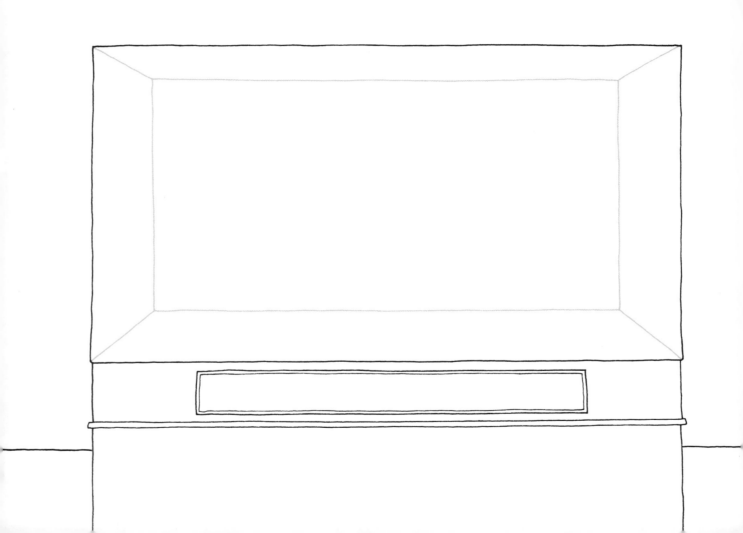

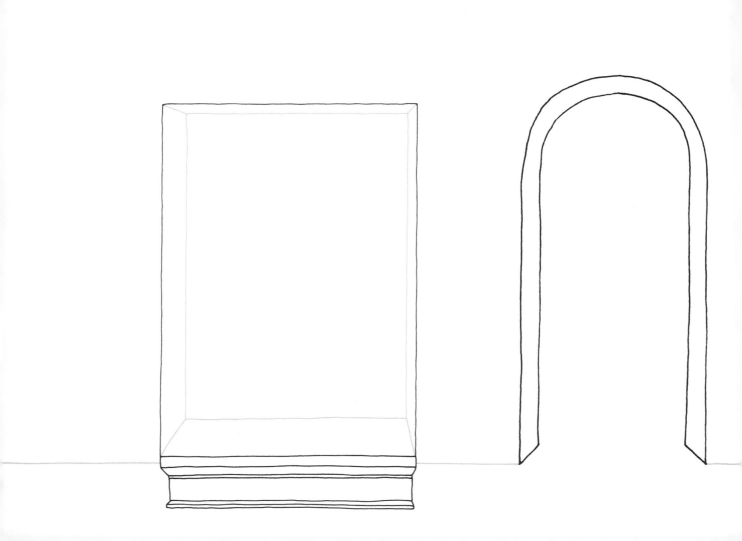

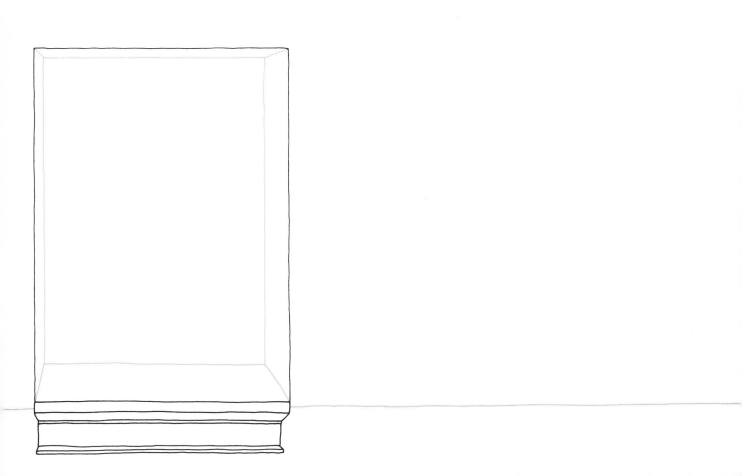

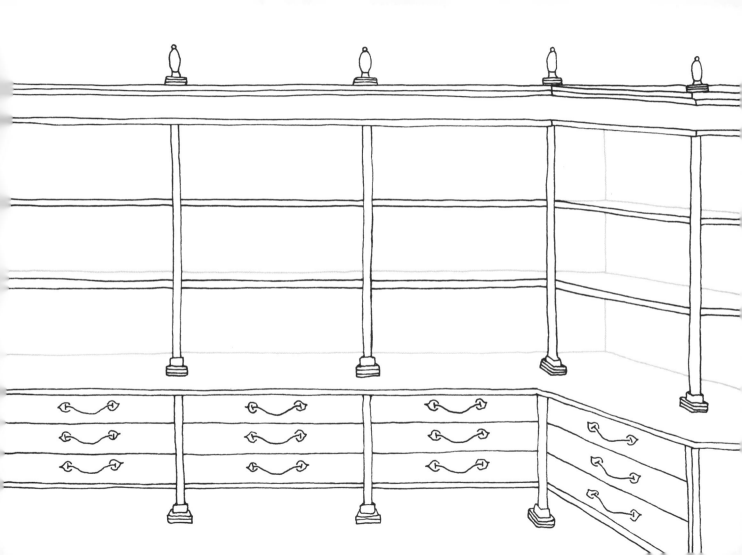

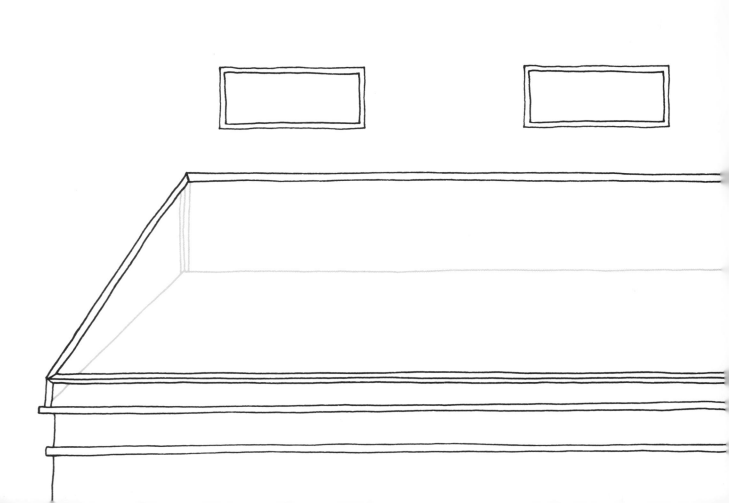

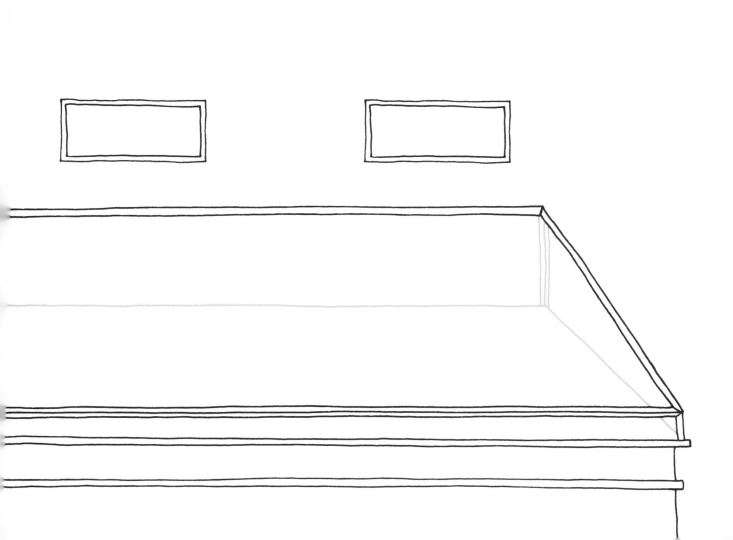

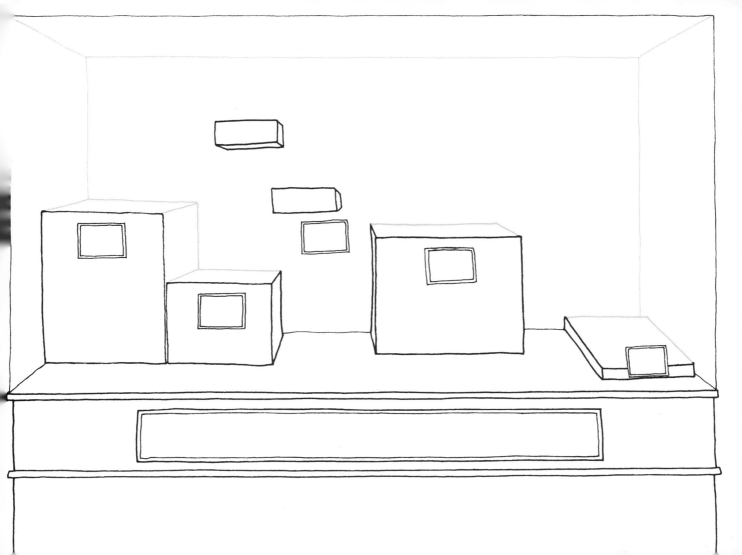

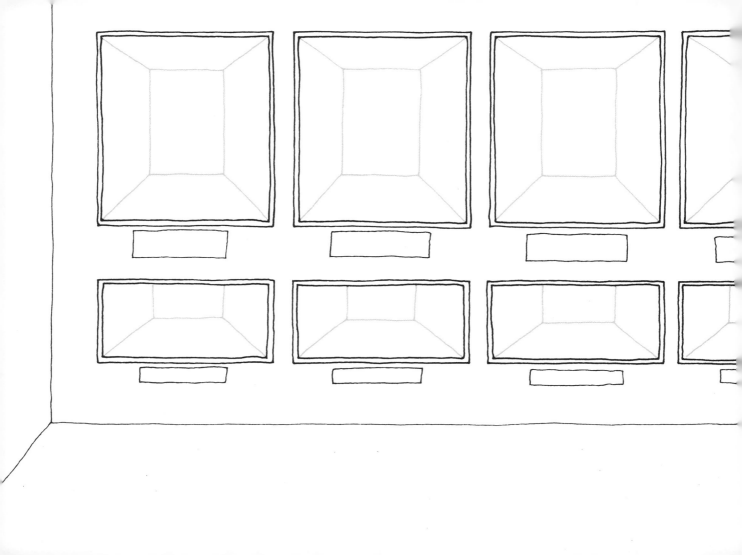

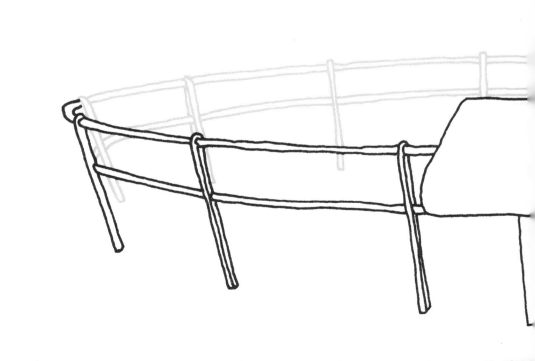

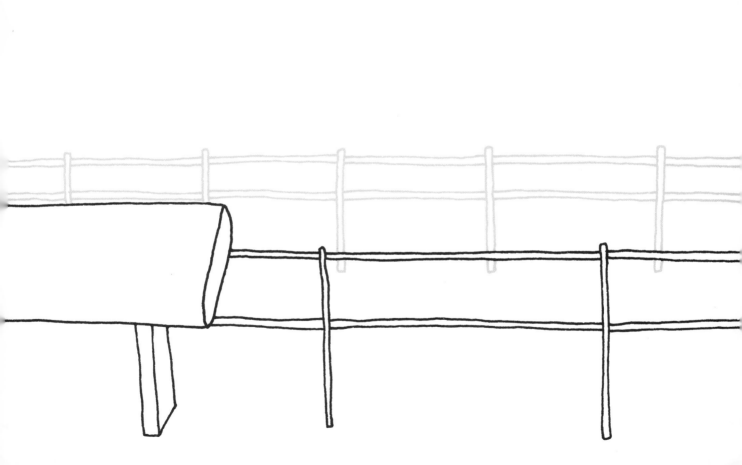

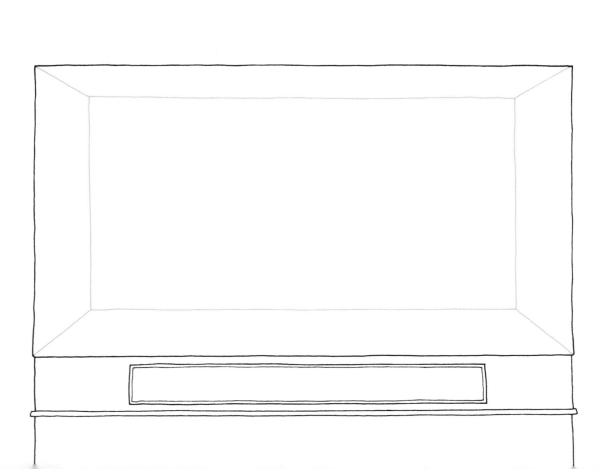

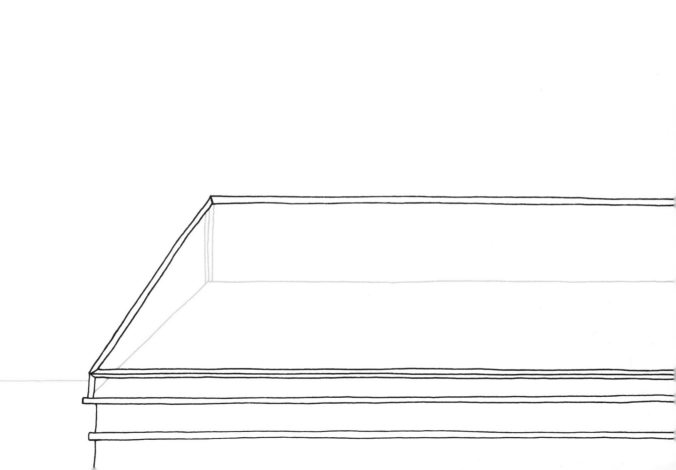

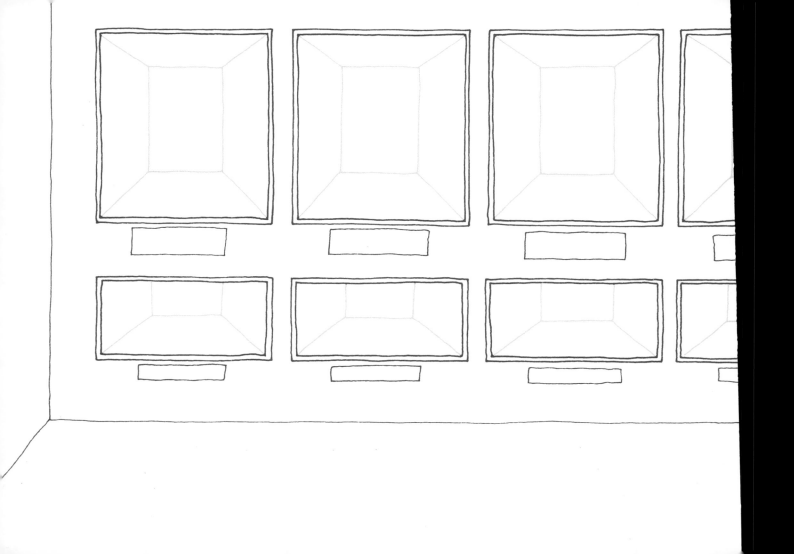

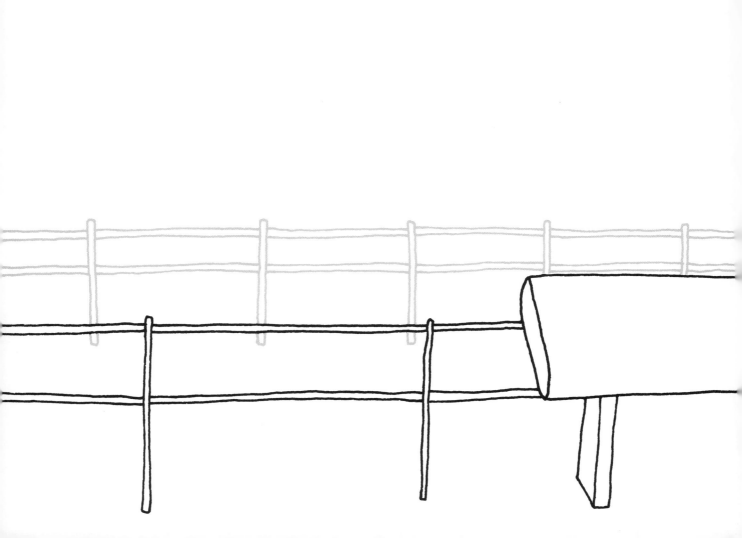

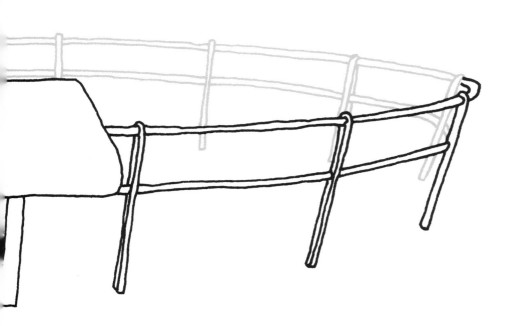

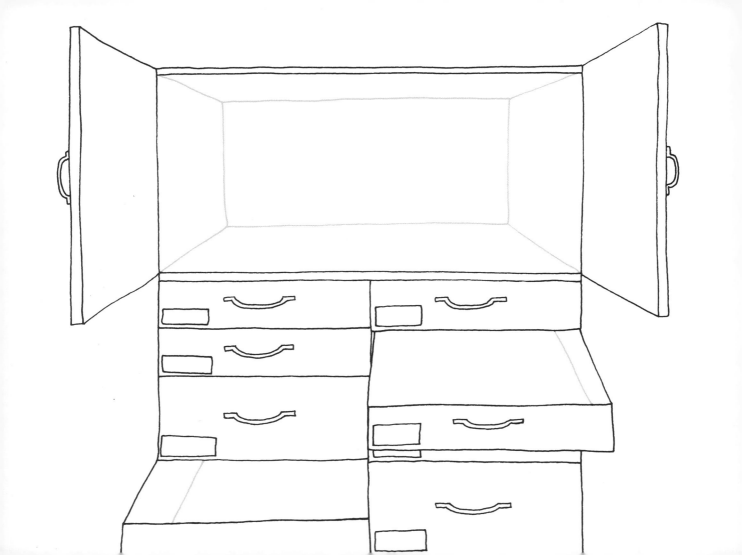

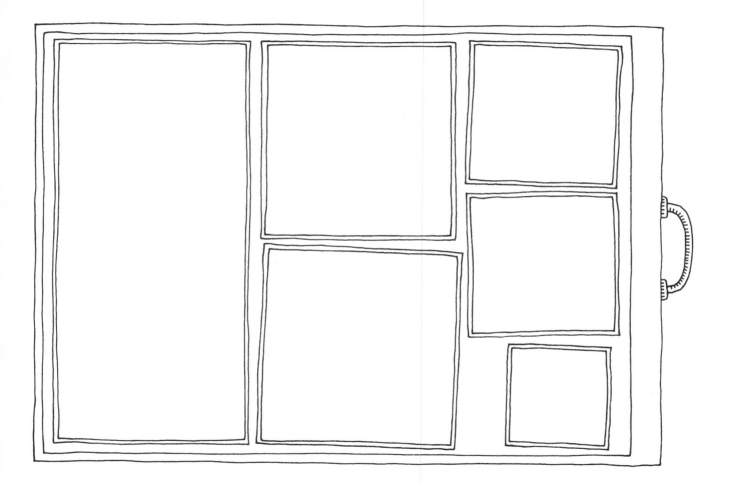

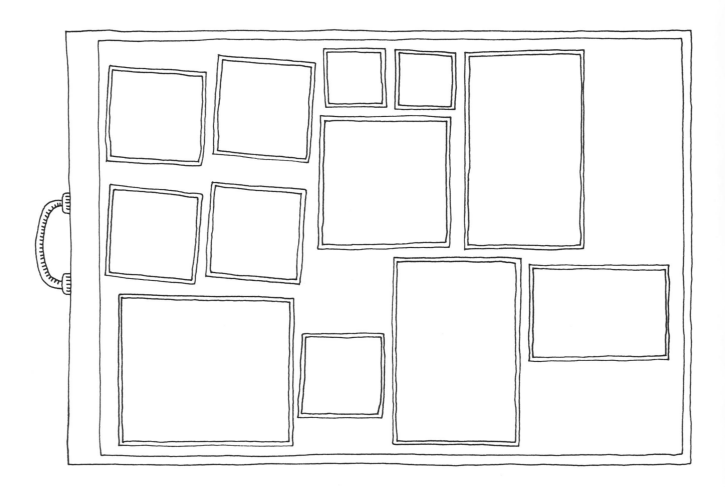

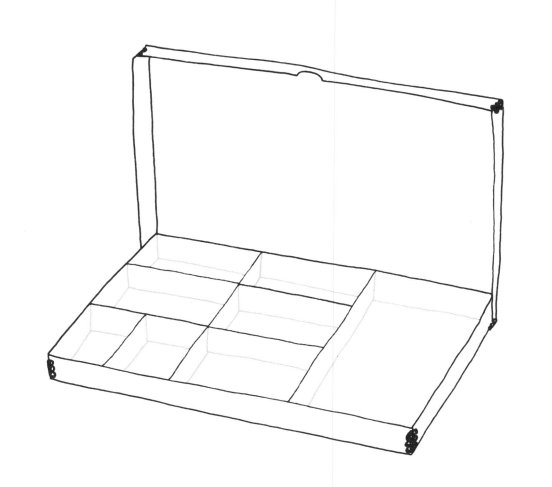

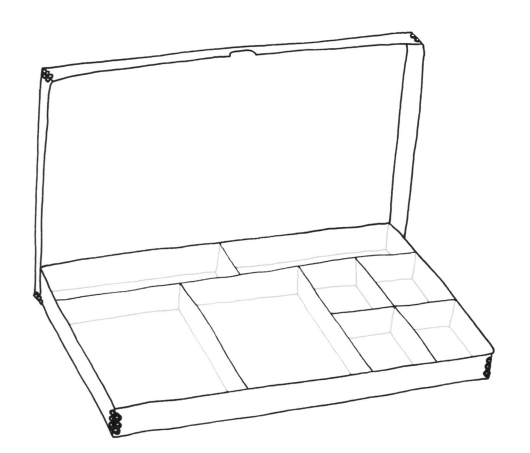

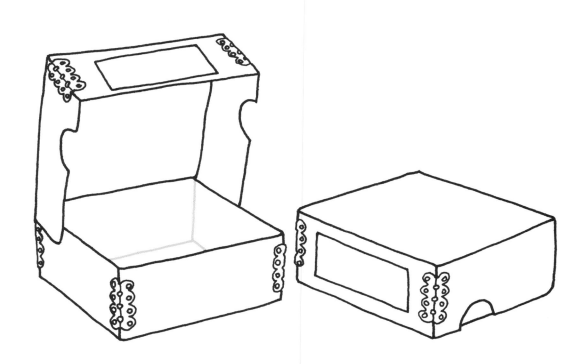

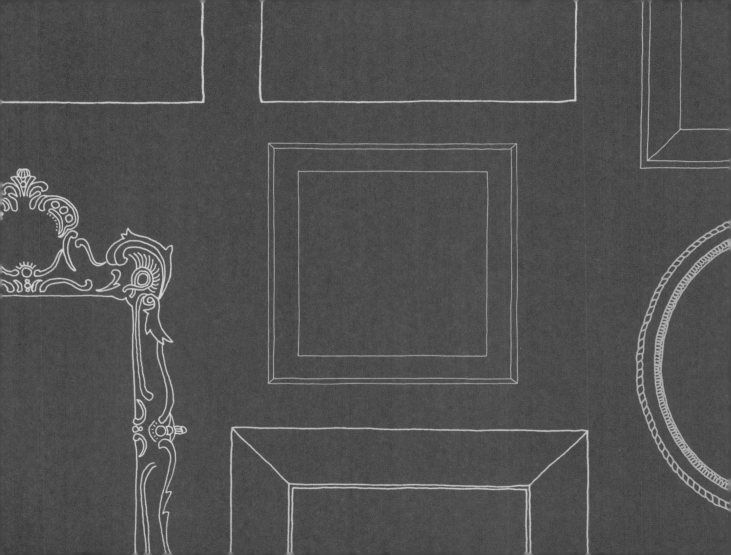